Low
Maintenance
Gardening

Low Maintenance Gardening

WRITER
ANNE M. ZEMAN

PHOTOGRAPHERS
ALAN COPELAND AND BARRY SHAPIRO

ILLUSTRATOR
JAMES BALKOVEK

AVON BOOKS ◆ NEW YORK

Product Manager: CYNTHIA FOLLAND, NK LAWN & GARDEN CO.

Acquisition, Development and Production Services:
BMR, Corte Madera, CA

Acquisition: JACK JENNINGS, BOB DOLEZAL

Series Concept: BOB DOLEZAL

Project Director: JANE RYAN

Developmental Editor: KATE KELLY

Horticulturist: BARBARA STREMPLE

Landscape Design and Horticultural Consultant: RG TURNER JR

Photographic Director: ALAN COPELAND

Art Director (cover): KARRYLL NASON

Art Director (interior): BRAD GREENE

Cover Design: KAREN EMERSON

Cover Styling: JOANN MASAOKA VAN ATTA

Cover Landscape Design: DENNIS TROMBURG ASSOCIATES, LANDSCAPE ARCHITECTS

Cover Photo: BARRY SHAPIRO

Interior Art: JAMES BALKOVEK

North American Map: RON HILDEBRAND

Landscape Plans: RG TURNER JR

Photo Assistant: LISA PISCHEL

Copy Editor: JANET VOLKMAN

Site Scout: PEGGY HENRY, RG TURNER JR, PAT TALBERT

Proofreader: LYNN FERAR

Typography and Page Layout: BARBARA GELFAND

Index: SYLVIA COATES

Color Separations: PREPRESS ASSEMBLY INCORPORATED

Printing and Binding: PENDELL PRINTING INC.

Production Management: THOMAS E. DORSANEO, JANE RYAN

First Avon Books Trade Printing: February 1993

Library of Congress Cataloging-in-Publication Data:
Zeman, Anne M.
  Low maintenance gardening / writer, Anne Zeman ;
  photographers Alan Copeland and Barry Shapiro ;
  illustrator James Balkovek.
    p. cm.
  Includes index.
  ISBN: 0-380-76804-6
  1. Landscape gardening. 2. Low maintenance
gardening. I. Copeland, Alan. II. Shapiro, Barry. III. Title.
SB473.Z46   1993
635.9–dc20   92-19074
                                              CIP

Special thanks to the following landscape designers for their assistance with sites: Patricia Posner, Kentfield, CA (pgs. 6–7); Peter Blustein (pgs. 30–31); Blue Sky Design Inc., Half Moon Bay, CA (pg. 31, dry stream bed); Cynthia Egger, Larkspur, CA (pgs. 40–41); Galen Fultz, Friends of the Garden, Mill Valley, CA (pgs. 68–69, Zebragrass). Also, San Benito House, Half Moon Bay, CA (pgs. 62–63).

Also thanks to: Strybing Arboretum & Botanical Garden and Golden Gate Park, San Francisco, CA; Roger Raiche; Blake Estate, UC Berkeley, CA; Maria Poindexter; Mary Beth and Kurt Reis; Rocky Marco; Miriam and Dick Dondero; Mary Jobson.

Notice: The information contained in this book is true and complete to the best of our knowledge. All recommendations are made without any guarantees on the part of the authors, NK Lawn & Garden Co., or BMR. Because the means, materials and procedures followed by homeowners are beyond our control, the author and publisher disclaim all liability in connection with the use of this information.

AVON BOOKS
A division of
The Hearst Corporation
1350 Avenue of the Americas
New York, New York 10019

AVON TRADEMARK REG. U.S. PAT. OFF.
AND IN OTHER COUNTRIES, MARCA
REGISTRADA, HECHO EN U.S.A.

92   93   94   95   96   10   9   8   7   6   5   4   3   2   1

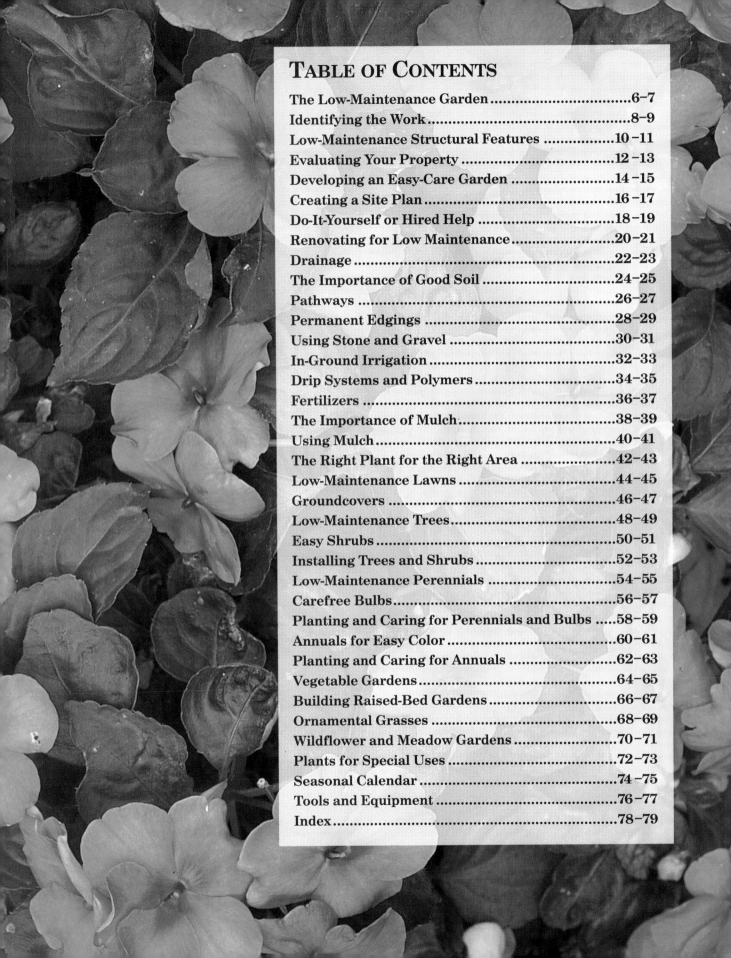

TABLE OF CONTENTS

THE LOW-MAINTENANCE GARDEN

Low Work, Not *No* Work

The ideal garden—an outdoor living space for playing, dining or just resting and enjoying the surroundings—would be maintenance free. But there is no way to eliminate all work and keep up a pleasant garden space. The lawn must be mowed, the plants watered and fertilized. Yet a low-maintenance garden, requiring minimal labor, allows most of the leisure of the work-free ideal.

A low-maintenance garden does not just happen; it is the result of careful planning. Take time to plan and install your low-maintenance garden. The hours and effort you put in up front will mean a minimum amount of time on maintenance and upkeep from that point on.

A low-maintenance garden doesn't mean a plain or unattractive garden. Quite the contrary—there are hundreds of trees, shrubs, and groundcovers from which to choose, many with flowering habits and colorful foliage. The secret is to use a combination that is labor-saving yet visually appealing.

The step-by-step instructions in this book will help you create your own low-maintenance environment, including tips for evaluating your property, designing your space, installing work-free features and selecting low-maintenance plants suitable to your personal tastes and local climate. Follow the guidelines, and your labor time will become leisure time spent lolling in a hammock or watching your garden grow.

IDENTIFYING THE WORK

EVALUATING MAINTENANCE NEEDS

The first thing you need to do is identify where the high-maintenance work is. Take a walk around your property with a notebook and make a list of all the chores you do in a given season. Consider how much time each area takes to maintain. Are there areas you would like to eliminate? Do you have a section that is visually appealing yet doesn't take much work? Can this be expanded? Which high-maintenance areas can be scaled down to reduce work?

Evaluate the plantings and determine which plants are the most labor intensive. Do you plant a vegetable garden every year? How often do you mow the lawn? Do you spend far too much time eliminating weeds?

After you take a good hard look at your property, decide which tasks you like to do and which are work, that is, the chores you hate performing. Rose gardens are a lot of work, but they may be the very thing you enjoy the most. You may have a passion for vegetables, which also require some special attention. If you have little interest in gardening, you will want to streamline maintenance in every way possible. Decide how much work you are willing to do and make a list, prioritizing what you wish to keep and what you wish to eliminate. This list will help you determine your gardening goals.

Roses are work-intensive, requiring watering, fertilizing, weeding, spraying, mulching, pruning and winterizing.

Beautiful large lawns require regular watering, mowing, trimming and weed control.

Certain types of trees are messy and require cleanup.

Beds and borders need watering, fertilizing, weeding, cultivating and deadheading.

Hedges need regular trimming.

LOW-MAINTENANCE STRUCTURAL FEATURES

Low-maintenance features, such as decks, patios, walkways and walls, allow you easy access to your garden while reducing space often devoted to high-maintenance gardening.

Fences, terraces and walls define your property, yet provide privacy and need less work than hedges.

Pathways and walks can be decorative as well as functional.

Decks and terraces, while reducing lawn space and maintenance, are perfect for entertaining or just lounging.

WORK-FREE FEATURES TO ENJOY

Planning a low-maintenance garden means replacing extensive lawn space or other high-maintenance areas with low-maintenance features. Structures, such as terraces, decks, fences, mowing strips, walkways or storage areas are virtually work free once installed.

Garden structures should be functional as well as beautiful. Choose materials for garden structures carefully, weighing each for its maintenance needs, appearance and cost. Select the highest quality materials you can afford—they last longer and require less maintenance. Find out about care requirements of materials—how long they last, how easy they are to clean and if they will need to be weatherproofed.

Brick and stone are sturdy materials that last the longest and require the least maintenance. Brick is excellent for constructing terraces, walkways, mowing strips and walls. It is attractive, comes in a variety of colors and sizes and can be set in a multitude of patterns.

Poured concrete makes durable and long-lasting steps and walkways. Concrete pavers, used like bricks, are less expensive. Stone and clay tiles, too, are popular materials for paving.

Because wood is subject to deterioration by weather, soil contact and insect attacks, choose decay-resistant lumber, such as redwood, cedar or cypress. Pressure-treated lumber is also used for decks. Railroad ties are used to build garden pavings, planters or fences. Although attractive and long-lasting, all wood features will decompose over time.

EVALUATING YOUR PROPERTY

Decks, patios and terraces should be constructed of minimum-maintenance materials.

Permanent structures reduce lawn size and so decrease mowing chores.

Raised beds for annuals and vegetables are easier to maintain.

Walkways should be made of durable materials and set flush with the lawn for easy mowing.

In-ground irrigation system will reduce time spent watering.

A salad garden can be small, producing no more than a family can use.

Fences provide privacy and security.

Avoid trees that drop blossoms, buds, fruits and seeds.

Groundcovers are virtually work free and are an excellent alternative to lawns.

For foundation plantings, choose slow-growing dwarf evergreens or low-growing, free-form shrubs. This will reduce trimming and keep plants from blocking light from windows.

PERSONAL CHECKLIST FOR LOW MAINTENANCE

Make a list of your landscaping goals. First determine what you want to eliminate or overhaul. Then make a list of projects. Here's a sample list:

- Remove vines and brambles from the back corner.
- Replace overgrown foundation shrubs covering front windows with dwarf varieties of evergreens that grow slowly and need little or no trimming.
- Remove privet hedge from property line and create an evergreen screen or install fence for privacy.
- Remove messy fruiting tree near the driveway. Replace with low-maintenance tree.
- Replace small front lawn space with groundcovers.
- Remove decaying woodpile and replace with play area for children, installing a 12 inch deep sand groundcovering.
- Put in a shrub border of low-maintenance shrubs of different heights, textures and bloom times.
- Plant work-free bulbs for color in the front and along the drive.
- For the area near the patio, choose a shade tree that needs little or no maintenance.
- Reduce work under trees and shrubs and along walkways by installing groundcover.
- Mulch all planting beds.
- Build raised beds to simplify care of annuals, herbs and vegetables.
- Minimize the size of your rear lawn and simplify the shape to facilitate mowing.

Developing an Easy-Care Garden

Setting Priorities

Plan the garden for your property carefully to ensure time, labor and expense will be kept to a minimum after installation. As you plan, set priorities.

First, measure the layout of your property (see pgs. 16–17). This overall view of the property together with your list of existing high-maintenance areas will help you decide what to overhaul or eliminate. High-maintenance trees, shrubs or overgrown areas should be removed before building any structures or installing equipment.

Next, decide on structural elements. Where do you want the sitting area or deck? Do you want overhanging or built-in planters? Do you need the privacy fence around the entire property? Prioritize the installation of structural elements according to your pocketbook, building the deck this year and the privacy fence next year.

Installing an in-ground irrigation system or a drip system will be the next physical priority. Before you can lay pipes, you need to determine where plantings will go and so tailor the system to your specific needs— lawns, groundcover areas and shrub borders.

When determining your landscape needs, make sure you list all your choices, from layout, design and plant selections to irrigation, structural features and other construction elements. Then establish priorities based on your complete list.

ELEMENTS OF A LOW-MAINTENANCE GARDEN

Evaluate your property carefully to locate high-maintenance areas. Then consider overhauling these areas with low-maintenance alternatives.

- Keep paved areas flush with the lawn. Mowing is easier if driveways, walkways and patios are on the same level, and the need to trim is reduced or eliminated. Keep the shape of your lawn simple to speed mowing.

- Install brick or concrete mowing strips between lawns and planting areas to provide easy access with the lawn mower and keep borders well defined.

- Use minimum-maintenance materials, such as concrete, flagstone, brick or stone for terrace, patio and walkways.

- Install an in-ground irrigation system or a drip system with automatic timers. These are more efficient and less time-consuming than portable sprinklers.

- Use mulches plentifully. Organic mulches keep soil moist, reduce the need to water and keep weeds down.

- Pave areas where foot traffic is heavy with concrete, stone or gravel.

- Keep flower beds narrow to keep maintenance manageable.

- Use the best possible soil for planting. Good soil is essential for healthy plants.

- Choose low-maintenance plants that are adaptable to your conditions and climate.

- Plant low-maintenance shrubs instead of a flower border.

CREATING A SITE PLAN

MEETING YOUR NEEDS

A good site plan includes the proper balance of plants, lawns and house and cannot be produced without careful organization and thought. Start with a deed map that shows the dimensions of your house and property. Verify the measurements and add distances to anything not pictured on the map. Be sure to include all permanent structures. Draw the plan to scale on graph paper using one-quarter inch for two feet. Make several copies of this drawing so that you can try different variations in design before making a final plan.

Divide your property into three areas: public , private and service. The public area is visible from the street and should look tidy and welcoming. Groundcovers, easy-care shrubs and a small lawn are useful elements here. The private area is devoted to the family's activities—a play area for children, entertainment and barbecue sections and any hobby gardens. Shrub borders and flower gardens can be used to set off these areas. If vegetable or rose beds are required, add these here. Be sure to include fences or hedges for privacy screens. The last section, the service area, is the portion dedicated to garbage, compost or deliveries. This is best screened in some fashion.

When you've plotted and selected plantings and structures to add or alter from your draft plans, incorporate all the elements into one master site plan.

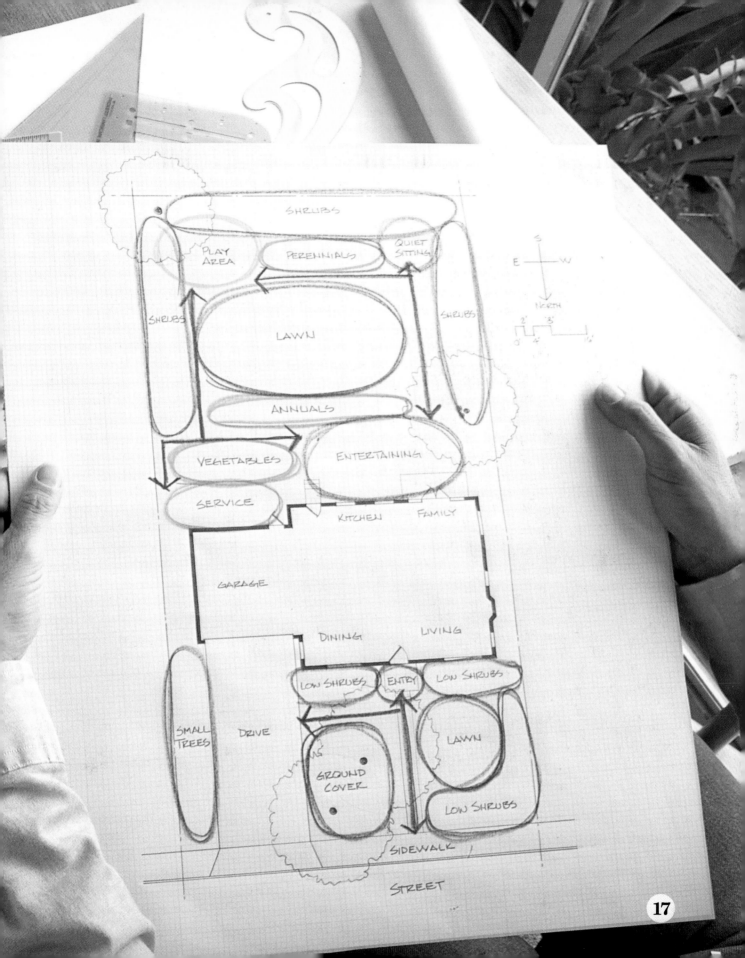

SHRUBS

PLAY AREA

PERENNIALS

QUIET SITTING

S

E — W

NORTH

SHRUBS

LAWN

SHRUBS

2' 3'

0' 4' 16'

ANNUALS

VEGETABLES

ENTERTAINING

SERVICE

KITCHEN

FAMILY

GARAGE

DINING

LIVING

LOW SHRUBS

ENTRY

LOW SHRUBS

SMALL TREES

DRIVE

LAWN

GROUND COVER

LOW SHRUBS

SIDEWALK

STREET

17

Do-It-Yourself or Hired Help

Making a Choice

So you've decided that you want to renovate for low maintenance. If you have the time and the inclination to do it yourself, none of the chores is difficult, but many are time-consuming. Some projects can be completed in a weekend or two, depending on your landscape goals, but installing both an irrigation system and a new deck can take several weekends. If you don't have the time or the inspiration, consider hiring a professional.

First, decide what you want to have done. If you are unsure of what needs to be done, get professional advice. The list on the right will help you determine who can best meet your needs. Ask for a consultation and estimate. And, of course, it's always recommended to get more than one opinion.

Although an additional expense, professional help is often well worth the extra dollars. Many professionals offer knowledge and experience in identifying and solving problems; they have large, sophisticated equipment and crews to tackle jobs quickly and effectively; and most offer guarantees. The biggest asset may be the time they save you from doing the work yourself.

Professional Help

If you've made the decision to hire a professional, make sure you understand what type of help each professional offers. Always insist on a contract that clearly outlines the terms and services to be performed and ask for references.

Landscape architects have a landscape architectural degree, and most states require a license. They can provide an overall plan that includes site planning, building codes, land-use laws, grading and drainage plan, irrigation, construction and lighting. They can also provide a planting plan. They usually charge a fee for a consultation.

Landscape designers are unlicensed but may have the same training as landscape architects. They can provide an overall garden design and planting plan. Often, they deal more with plants and living elements and less with permanent structures. Their expertise may vary; because they are unlicensed they may not be able to file building permits.

Garden designers are another step removed from the landscape architect. They usually specialize in selecting and installing beds and borders.

Landscape contractors are trained to install landscapes. In most states, a license is required. They can grade, repair drainage problems, prepare soil and install water systems. Most install permanent structures, such as decks, patios, fences or walls.

Landscapers, a catch-all term, may refer to the above-mentioned professionals, but usually means those who do traditional yard work, such as lawn maintenance, pruning and planting. Landscapers install shrubs or borders, but, unless you are familiar with their work, they should not be used for design. They are not licensed.

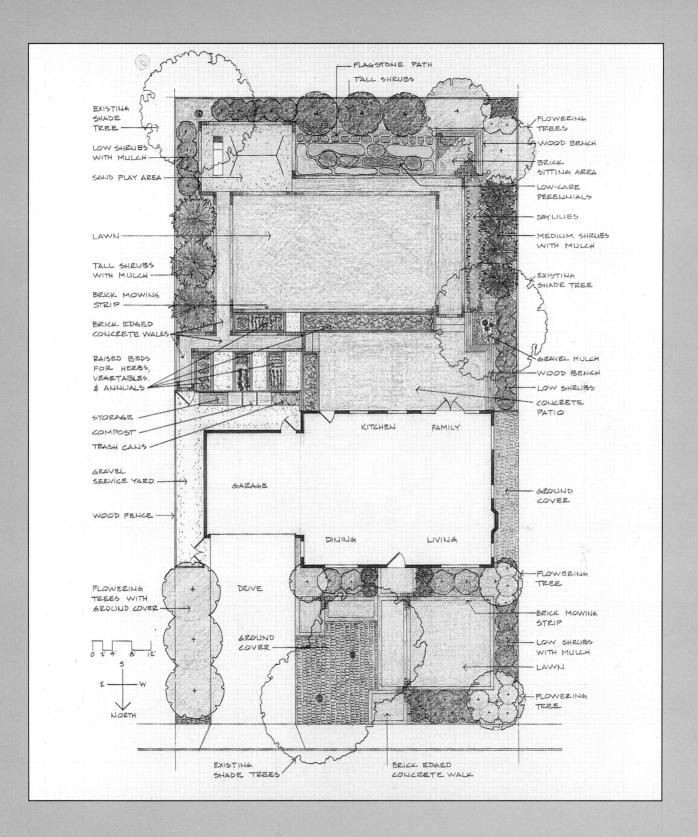

EXISTING SHADE TREE

LOW SHRUBS WITH MULCH

SAND PLAY AREA

LAWN

TALL SHRUBS WITH MULCH

BRICK MOWING STRIP

BRICK EDGED CONCRETE WALKS

RAISED BEDS FOR HERBS, VEGETABLES, & ANNUALS

STORAGE

COMPOST

TRASH CANS

GRAVEL SERVICE YARD

WOOD FENCE

FLOWERING TREES WITH GROUND COVER

GROUND COVER

FLAGSTONE PATH

TALL SHRUBS

FLOWERING TREES

WOOD BENCH

BRICK SITTING AREA

LOW-CARE PERENNIALS

DAYLILIES

MEDIUM SHRUBS WITH MULCH

EXISTING SHADE TREE

GRAVEL MULCH

WOOD BENCH

LOW SHRUBS

CONCRETE PATIO

GROUND COVER

FLOWERING TREE

BRICK MOWING STRIP

LOW SHRUBS WITH MULCH

LAWN

FLOWERING TREE

KITCHEN   FAMILY

GARAGE

DINING   LIVING

DRIVE

0 2' 4'   8'   12'

S

E — W

NORTH

EXISTING SHADE TREES

BRICK EDGED CONCRETE WALK

19

RENOVATING FOR LOW MAINTENANCE

PLANNING RENOVATIONS

Renovating for low maintenance is sometimes as easy as replacing shrubs or taking out a tree. But, it usually means something more substantial like installing an in-ground irrigation system, building a deck, replacing flower beds with easy-care shrubs or decreasing the size of your lawn.

Use your list of high-maintenance chores to determine where the most important work is. Bear in mind that renovating for low maintenance means doing work now to reduce on-going labor in the long run.

If your lawn requires the most maintenance now, consider replacing part of it with a deck or patio. On sloping or shady sections, put in a groundcover that thrives with very little care. Or install pathways and walks that divide the lawn into smaller, manageable areas. If watering is time-consuming in your region, look into in-ground irrigation systems that operate automatically and use water more efficiently. If your lawn needs replacing, select a grass type that needs less water and mowing.

If foundation plantings need constant trimming, watering and weeding, you can replace them with other, less demanding shrubs. Select plants carefully, though, as they differ widely in care requirements. And take the time now to prepare the soil thoroughly, with amendments that improve its structure and nutrients. Healthy plants, in good soil, always require less care than sickly ones.

SOLUTIONS TO HIGH-MAINTENANCE PROBLEMS

Problem: Lawn is too large and time-consuming to maintain.

Solution: Determine if the lawn in its current form serves a purpose. If possible, scale down the lawn to a smaller mowing area by installing a deck, patio or terrace; or, create a shrub border and make use of groundcovers and mulch around trees. Lawns could also be turned into wild areas, such as prairies with native wildflowers and shrubs.

Problem: Flower beds or borders of annuals and perennials require a lot of watering, weeding and replanting.

Solution: Replace with low-maintenance perennials or a shrub border that require less care; reduce the number of different kinds of plants to two or three; mulch to reduce watering.

Problem: Lawn grows poorly, if at all, under shady trees.

Solution: Replace with a groundcover, ferns or decorative stone or gravel. Under low-branching, full trees where grass struggles, plant a groundcover that performs in deep shade, such as periwinkle, pachysandra or ivy. Creating large beds around trees with groundcovers, stones or mulch will create an attractive look while reducing mowing.

Problem: Lawns are difficult to mow on steep slopes and terraces.

Solution: Avoid impossible-to-mow situations by using a low-maintenance groundcover on steep slopes, bumpy areas or terraces. Groundcovers will also check soil erosion.

Problem: Yew, box or privet hedges need regular maintenance and trimming.

Solution: Replace with less formal, free-form shrubs. If privacy is needed, install a low-maintenance fence. Vines grown along a fence can soften the look.

Problem: Weeds are widespread and constantly proliferating.

Solution: Make generous use of mulches to keep weeds down—the mulch also slows evaporation, reducing the need to water. For weeds growing between bricks and flagstones, replace soil and sand between bricks with mortar.

Problem: Trimming along paths or garden area often takes longer than mowing.

Solution: Install brick mowing strips or concrete strips between pavements or gardens and grass, making a flush area that the lawn mower can pass over easily and reduce or eliminate the need for trimming.

Problem: Vegetable garden requires constant attention and care.

Solution: Scale down the size of the garden. Set plants close together in raised beds and mulch generously to control weeds. Do not grow more than your family can use.

Problem: Moving and storing garden furniture every season has become too difficult.

Solution: Purchase or make permanent weatherproof seating out of decay-resistant woods, such as redwood or cedar.

DRAINAGE

Adequate drainage is required for most plants and is essential for proper soil aeration. Poor drainage can be improved by amending the soil. In addition, your property must have sufficient slope to carry off surface water so that it will not collect and cause damage to plants and grass.

First Dig a hole 1 ft. across and 2 ft. deep in your garden soil.

Then If the soil has been watered recently, cover the hole and surrounding soil with plastic and wait 7 days until the soil dries.

Next Fill the hole to the brim with water and begin timing.

Last If the water drains in less than 5 minutes, the soil is too sandy; if it takes more than 15 minutes, the soil has too much clay.

Building a Garden Drain

First Mark off the low area with garden lime or stake and string.

Then Dig a trench 16–24 in. deep, centered on the lowest spot, at a pitch of 3–4 in. per 100 ft., to a creek, storm drain or dry well. Fill the base of the trench with 2–3 in. of gravel.

Next Lay 4 in. diameter drain pipe with the perforation holes facing down.

Last Cover the pipe with gravel to a depth of 4 in. and tamp down the surface. Backfill the trench.

DRAINAGE PROBLEMS

Water is essential to plants, but it must be in a usable form. Just as the amount of rainfall varies greatly from one region to another, so does the ability of different garden soils to absorb water. Drainage can take place above ground, as surface run-off into ditches, streams or drains; or below ground, as infiltration down through the soil. If your soil surface is dry and hard, even a heavy rainfall will run off quickly, leaving little or no water to pass down into the ground. If your soil is wet and waterlogged, excess water will prevent air from reaching your plant roots, and the plants will eventually die.

Special drainage problems can occur when the topsoil is caked or when the native soil is stripped away to the subsoil, as often happens in excavation or new home construction. The exposed subsoil may be too compacted to permit water infiltration, or it may be so wet from a high water table that pumping or artificial drainage is needed.

A quick drainage test of your soil will reveal whether you have any such problems. Depending on your soil type, you can choose from among many different soil amendments to improve the workability and drainage of your soil.

Tube or tile drainage is the method for piping out excess water from low-lying areas. Larger gardens will need networks of tiles but small areas usually need only a single line of 4 inch diameter pipe running out to a ditch or sewer line.

THE IMPORTANCE OF GOOD SOIL

Types of Soil

Sandy Soil Sandy soil consists of large, individual mineral particles. It has a lot of air space and crumbles easily when squeezed. Roots penetrate it readily, but water and nutrients drain away quickly. Sandy soil is often called "light" soil.

Silt Soil Silt soil has small-sized mineral particles that are larger than clay and smaller than sand. When dry silt is squeezed, it breaks up and is lumpy. It retains water well, but lacks important air space between particles. Add organic matter to improve soil with too much silt.

Clay Soil Clay soil is made up of very tiny, flat mineral particles that are easily compacted. It is often called "heavy" soil, because it packs together densely, holding water and impairing drainage. Wet clay is sticky and holds firm. Dry clay is hard.

Loam Soil Often called the ideal soil, loam contains nearly equal parts of clay, silt and sand. It retains moisture, air and nutrients yet drains easily. It is also referred to as "loose" or "friable" soil.

Soil Amendments

Compost Compost is organic matter, such as leaves, grass clippings or vegetable waste, which has been sufficiently decomposed to form a rich, crumbly, dark soil. It is an excellent conditioner for clay, silt and sandy soils.

Peat Peat moss has superb water-holding ability and is excellent for sandy soils. It increases the acidity of the soil. Readily available commercially in bags, but often expensive.

UNDERSTANDING SOIL

All garden soils are mixtures of clay, silt and sand. Soils with too much clay are dense, hard to work with and drain poorly. Sandy soils are loose and dry out quickly. The best garden soils—loams—combined with decayed plant matter, are easy to work and hold water and air.

The most accurate way to determine the type of soil you have in your garden is to have it tested professionally. This can often be done by sending a soil sample to your Agricultural Extension Service, a local agency listed in the phone book.

The results of your soil test will show a complete soil analysis including a pH reading of your sample. PH is measured on a scale of 0–14, with the low end representing acidity and the high end alkalinity. A neutral to slightly acid soil of 6.5–7.0 is best.

Improve sandy and clay soils with organic matter, such as compost or well-rotted manure. If your soil is acidic, as it is in much of the East and Northwest, you may need to add an application of lime.

Much of the soil in the West and Southwest is alkaline. It can be neutralized by adding sulfur, gypsum or lime-sulfur. All are commonly available at your nursery.

Well-rotted Manure An excellent source of nutrients as well as a good soil conditioner. Do not use fresh manure, which is high in ammonia salts that can burn plants. Fresh manure should decay for 1 year before use in the garden.

PATHWAYS

PATHWAYS: ORNAMENTAL AND USEFUL

The basic function of a walk or garden path is to provide a route across and around your home and property. Walkways lead to your front door, to service areas and even to your garden bench. In the low-maintenance garden, walkways and stepping stones should be constructed of brick, stone, concrete or other durable material. They should also provide a nonskid surface for sure footing.

Walkways should be at least three feet across. Make them four to five feet wide for strolling side-by-side. Provide a good foundation to help walks last for many years.

The garden path should be aesthetically pleasing as well as functional. Rarely should paths be straight and narrow; varying the curve and the width of the walkway creates a range of perspectives. Gently curving paths can level out steeper climbs and present new, unexpected views of the garden. Sharp intersections and tight curves will feel uncomfortable.

Where the pathway cannot be conveniently curved to go around a slope, use wooden, stone or brick steps to adjust the level of the path to the new height. Steps should be uniform and slope forward slightly for drainage.

Building a Gravel Path

First Determine desired path width. Lay out the walkway using stakes and string. Dig trench 2 in. deep and install sturdy strip edging.

Next Fill with gravel 3/8 to 5/8 in. size to just below top of edging.

Last Smooth, tamp and level using a bow rake.

Types of Paths

Brick Brick paving can be arranged in a variety of patterns and designs.

Log Cuts Creating a natural look, log cuts are usually a 3 in. cross-section through the trunk of a tree and laid down in a stepping stone pattern.

Flagstones A favorite for paths and terraces, flagstones also make excellent stepping stones on a grass lawn.

Gravel Decorative gravel or crushed stone is inexpensive, useful and easy to maintain.

Bark Chips Wood chips create an informal look and are especially appropriate through woodland settings.

Stones Small river stones or field stones give a varied texture to the landscape and are easy to care for.

PERMANENT EDGINGS

Mowing strips eliminate the need to trim lawns by hand. Mower wheels can run on top of edging that is level with the soil. Use permanent edging to separate lawns from planting beds, groundcovers or trees to reduce maintenance.

Installing Strip Edgings

First Purchase steel, aluminum or polyethylene strip edging. Dig a trench as deep as the width of the edging between lawn and planting area.

Then Place the edging just above the root zone of the grass, level with the top of the soil.

Next Stake the edging in place.

Last Backfill and level, leaving soil 1 in. lower on the planting side.

USING STRIP EDGINGS

Installing permanent landscape edging is an easy and inexpensive step in reducing yard work. Edging keeps your landscape looking neat and well maintained by defining the boundaries between lawn and garden areas. Barriers are formed to prevent grass and weeds from spreading into gardens and over walkways. Edging helps contain mulch such as bark chips and stone, and limits the need for trimming after mowing.

The best edging materials are strips of manufactured edging made of steel, polyethylene or heavy-duty aluminum. All of these will last years with minimum or no maintenance. Edgings made of two inch thick plywood, thin corrugated aluminum or decorative scalloped cinder blocks are also available, but are not as easy to maintain and may be difficult to mow around.

Installing edging is not a difficult job, but should be done with care. Be sure that all edgings are staked to secure them in place. Many products indicate that this is not necessary, but don't be fooled. This is particularly important if you live in areas where the ground freezes and thaws in the winter, forcing the edging out of the ground.

Steel is the easiest to work with for straight lines and level ground. If you live in an area with moist, acid soil, steel will deteriorate faster. Polyethylene and aluminum last for years, but may require more work to install. Polyethylene is more flexible and better for curving lines or tight areas.

Other materials can be used for attractive lawn edging, such as bricks laid end up. Unusual or interesting stones can work nicely, but do not save time as do flat mowing strips.

USING STONE AND GRAVEL

Stones, river rocks and gravel add low-maintenance advantages as well as beauty to your garden. Easy to use and inexpensive, they make an attractive alternative to groundcovers.

How to Install River Rocks

First Install edging to keep stones in place and for ease of mowing.

Next Lay fabric weed barrier.

Last Put in river stones deep enough so that the weed barrier does not show.

GROUNDCOVER ALTERNATIVES

The use of gravel as a groundcover began to increase with its popularity in Japanese gardens. Creating a calm beauty, the Japanese make artful use of sand, gravel, stones and rocks. While Japanese gardens are often time-consuming to maintain, the use of gravel and stones as groundcovers is an extremely low-maintenance idea.

Using gravel and stone can bring another texture to your landscape. Smooth stones from riverbeds make an attractive wide basin around a tree; or use crushed gravel as a mulch around the foundation plantings or shrub borders. Gravel can be an inexpensive groundcover, useful and easy to maintain. It is an excellent mulch where cultivation is not necessary and comes in a variety of shapes, sizes and colors.

An excellent use of river-washed rocks is a dry stream—that is, the use of rocks and gravel to create a natural stream look, but without water. Often, a dry stream can conceal a natural drainage channel. It has visual beauty and creates drama in the landscape.

When making use of gravel and stone as a groundcover, use it judiciously. An entire "lawn" of green gravel in the front of your house requires little maintenance but is very artificial in appearance.

In-Ground Irrigation

PLANNING A SYSTEM

Underground automatic sprinkler systems are easy to use and efficient.

Basic parts include an automatic timer, control valves, pipes and pipe fittings, sprinkler heads, risers, anti-siphon valves and drain-out valves, necessary if your area freezes in winter. Prior to designing your system, locate underground utility lines. Avoid trenching near lines.

First test your water pressure, then map your system in a scale drawing. Workbooks are available along with free advice at many lawn centers. Plot lines and sprinklers along the perimeter of your lawn, with quarter-circle sprinkler heads in the corners, half-circle heads along the edges and, if needed, full-circle heads in the middle. Overlap every head's spray pattern for even coverage. Make a separate circuit for each area or group of sprinklers.

Once you've planned the type and number of sprinklers, purchase pipe and all components. Dig trenches 8–12 inches deep, either by hand or with a trenching machine. Cut pipe sections to length and lay out the whole system in the trenches with loose joints before applying any glue. When everything fits correctly, join them together with primer and glue.

Next, install sprinkler risers of the correct height. Then build the manifold and tap into the main service line, as described on the next page. Before attaching the sprinkler heads, flush the system of dirt and debris by running water through it.

In areas with freezing temperatures, be sure to install a self-draining valve at the lowest part of the system.

Installing the System

First Test your water pressure. Water line pressure must be at least 20 PSI (pressure per sq. in.). Use a pressure gauge, available at lawn centers and plumbing supply stores.

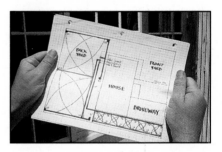

Then Using graph paper, draw system with overlapping spray to allow for even coverage. No circuit should exceed the gallons per minute available at the main service. List and buy all materials, consulting with your lawn center specialist.

Third Dig a trench, assemble valves in advance and install the valve system, including anti-siphon valves. Check for leaks.

Fourth Mark the layout of your system and location of heads with stakes and string. Dig V-shaped trenches by hand or use a trenching machine.

Next Assemble by cutting pipe with hacksaw and gluing PVC pipe with solvent. Check that local codes allow use of PVC pipe. Use copper pipe in freeze zones. Wait 1 hour, then flush to clear any debris before installing sprinkler heads.

Last Check coverage, adjust sprinkler heads and backfill trenches. Prepare area for planting.

CONTROLS AND MANIFOLDS

Each sprinkler circuit has its own control valve, operated manually or electrically by an automatic timer. The control valves should be placed together in a manifold, with each connected to its circuit on one side and to the main water supply line on the other.

An anti-siphon valve on every circuit stops sprinkler water from draining into your household drinking water.

To tap into the supply line, turn off the house water at the meter. Cut the supply pipe, and install a compression tee and shutoff valve. Follow all applicable building codes for your area. If you have a water softener, always install sprinklers between the softener and the meter. Then attach the tee to the sprinkler supply line and manifold. Use the same method to tap into basement or existing outside faucet lines.

Drip Systems and Polymers

Installing Drip Irrigation

Planning Water Systems

Watering is the most demanding and essential garden chore. During long, dry spells it may be needed daily. The ideal solution for the low-maintenance gardener is an in-ground irrigation system as described on pgs. 32–33; but these are costly and may not be needed for smaller areas or in parts of the country where rain is plentiful. There are many alternatives to the in-ground system—drip systems, soaker hoses and various types of sprinklers.

Drip systems are low maintenance and efficient water delivery systems. You can position water delivery heads wherever you need them, and you can tailor the system to large or small areas. Plus, drip lines can be above ground and are made of flexible plastic; therefore, the layout can be easily rearranged as the landscape changes.

Drip irrigation operates at low water pressure, maintaining a gentle flow at the ground level and requiring less water than standard sprinkler systems. The volume of water delivered to each plant is controlled by the number of emitters and the gallons per hour (gph) capacity of the emitters. Drip irrigation is excellent for relatively widely spaced shrubs and trees or uniformly spaced plants, such as hedges.

Porous soaker hoses also use low pressure, spreading water by means of tiny holes in their tubing. They can be attached to a regular garden hose for installation above or under ground. They are useful for watering plants set out in rows, such as in vegetable gardens, and in densely planted flower beds.

First For easy installation, begin your drip irrigation set up by attaching a "Y" to the faucet. The drip system will operate off one side, and you can connect a hose to the other. Use Teflon tape or pipe joint compound on this and all threaded connections to prevent leaks.

Then Attach an anti-siphon backflow preventer, a pressure regulator and a hose to pipe connector. The backflow preventer keeps irrigation water from draining into the household water. Be sure this element has a screen washer or add a separate filter to keep debris out of the lines. The pressure regulator allows the system to operate at a constant low pressure so water is evenly distributed. The 1/2 in. main tubing will be fitted into the connector.

Third Unroll the 1/2 in. tubing and distribute it throughout the garden. Lay it in a shallow trench and anchor it down with pins. Punch holes in the tubing where you want feeder lines to run to plants or where micro sprinklers are desired. Use a special punch designed for drip systems. Cover the main tubing after all connections are made and checked.

Last Insert connectors into the holes, and attach the feeder lines. When all emitters, sprinklers and sprayers are connected to feeder lines, turn the system on and flush out any dirt or debris. Push the emitters onto the ends of the feeder lines, and position them at the base of the plants. If desired, bury this line as well. Then cap off the 1/2 in. tubing to pressurize the system. Regularly check individual emitters, clean filters and flush the lines to prevent clogging.

WATER-ABSORBING POLYMERS

Relatively new to the market are water-absorbing, polymer-based gels that, when put into the soil, act like sponges, holding water so you can irrigate less frequently.

Research is still on going about the long-term effectiveness of these compounds, but they are commercially available now at most garden centers. The polymers are easy to use. Simply dig a hole in the soil, put the recommended amount of gel into it and mix well with the soil. Plants send feeder roots into the polymer and can tap into the the water held there. Be sure to read the label instructions and follow accordingly.

Polymers save you time and effort in watering. They are particularly useful for plants in containers, which tend to dry out quickly in summer heat and require almost daily watering. With polymers, these plants will stay moist for several days.

Your local garden center or nursery can help you decide the best usage of polymers to suit the plants in your garden.

FERTILIZERS

SLOW-RELEASE FERTILIZERS FOR MINIMUM CARE

Making use of slow-release fertilizers can save the gardener time. Slow-release fertilizers are specially formulated to release their nutrients gradually over a period of weeks or months. They often come in pellet form and are also called "controlled-release." They reduce the need for frequent, repeated applications of fertilizer.

Slow-release fertilizers can be used for trees, lawns, borders, shrubs and bulbs. They are ideal for container plants. Because containers and hanging baskets have less soil to draw nutrients from and require more frequent waterings than plants in the ground, nutrients leach out of the soil quickly. Feeding with regular fertilizer is usually needed once a week in this case. One application of slow-release fertilizer will feed the plant for three to six months.

Lawns also benefit from slow-release fertilizers. Each application supplies your lawn with several months of a constant rate of nutrients at a lower level of concentration than normal liquid and powder fertilizers. When purchasing pellets for the lawn, look for a fertilizer that contains 25–30 percent of its nitrogen in a slow- or controlled-release form.

Slow-release fertilizer pellets make nutrients available to plants over several months.

Place slow-release fertilizer pellets or tablets in the bottom of the prepared hole before planting trees. For trees already in the ground, bury pellets about 3–6 in. below the surface. Be sure to read the label instructions and follow accordingly.

ORGANIC AND INORGANIC FERTILIZERS

The principal ingredients of fertilizers are nitrogen, phosphorous and potassium, or NPK. Nitrogen is responsible for green, vegetative growth and foliage. Phosphorous helps develop roots and flowers. Potassium contributes to the plant's strength and overall metabolism. Different fertilizers include different proportions of these three nutrients; it is important to match the fertilizer you use with the specific needs of plants.

Fertilizers come in either organic or synthetic forms. Organic fertilizers, sometimes called "natural organic," are those that are derived from plants, animals or minerals, such as manure, bone meal and fish emulsion. They release nutrients slowly, and often contribute positively to a soil's structure. An organic substance—such as manure—used alone, however, is not always completely balanced in NPK. Recently, though, manufacturers have developed so-called blended organics, which are prepackaged in the NPK ratio you desire, eliminating guesswork.

Synthetic, or chemically processed, fertilizers include readily available packaged fertilizers that have the NPK proportion balanced and marked on the container. They have the advantages of premixed proportions, compact storage and low cost. They are made to release their nutrients quickly, however, so need to be reapplied often. Also, it is wise to follow label directions carefully, as these substances can burn plants.

Both organic and synthetic fertilizers come in dry and liquid forms. Dry fertilizers dissolve with each watering. Liquids are applied with a hose-end sprayer or watering can and start to work immediately, but they don't last long and are generally more expensive.

THE IMPORTANCE OF MULCH

BENEFITS OF MULCH

Mulch is the low-maintenance gardener's secret weapon. A good mulch can greatly reduce the amount of time and labor required for maintenance, plus it improves plant growth.

The greatest advantage of using mulch is the conservation of moisture in the soil. A proper mulch allows water to penetrate into the soil but it reduces the rate of evaporation due to sunlight and exposure by providing a protective blanket between the elements and the soil surface. Rain can be absorbed through mulch but does not pack the surface. During heavy rains, mulch keeps the surface from eroding and permits rain to seep in more slowly.

One of the strongest arguments for mulch is weed control. A two to three inch layer of mulch eliminates the need for hours of tiresome weeding. In fact, few weeds can push their way through a thick mulch, and those that do can be easily removed.

Mulch also lowers soil temperature and keeps it uniform. This is particularly useful in the summer when intense heat could destroy roots close to the surface. This insulation may cool the soil temperature by as much as 20°F.

Organic mulches eventually break down into humus improving structure and texture of soil. The process of decomposition releases nutrients and adds to the fertility of the soil.

Compost Create an excellent mulch and soil conditioner from your own garden with shredded leaves, grass clippings and vegetable waste from the kitchen.

Wood Chips Effective and attractive, but nitrogen will need to be supplemented, as decomposing chips take nitrogen from the soil.

Rice Hulls Light, easy-to-use and weed free, but tend to blow away in windy areas.

Mushroom Compost Fine mulch but often difficult to find, except where mushrooms are farmed. Also makes an excellent soil amendment.

Cocoa Shells Attractive color, highly absorbent and lend a wonderful chocolate smell the first week. Readily available wherever chocolate is made.

Shredded Leaves Excellent soil conditioner and mulch. Whole leaves tend to mat and mold when wet.

ORGANIC AND INORGANIC MULCHES

Mulches are various materials used on the ground around plants to conserve moisture, keep down weeds and prevent soil erosion. They are either organic or inorganic.

Organic mulches are the most common mulches. Almost any organic waste material can be used for mulching but choose one that will also be attractive in the home garden. Decaying mulch materials add nutrients to the soil and help preserve the structure of a soil by preventing a hard crust from forming on the surface. Many organic mulches, such as compost, shredded leaves and hay break down to form humus. Wood chips, rice hulls and cocoa shells make some of the most attractive organic mulches and are easy to use and apply.

Decorative stones and gravel, river rocks and black plastic are usually referred to as inorganic mulches. They provide the same function as organic mulches, but they do not decompose, and they do not provide any nutrients to the plants. Inorganic mulches are more permanent and do not have to be replaced as often.

When selecting a mulch, consider the availability of the material, the cost, the benefit to the soil, the appearance, its durability, how quickly it decomposes and how comparatively weed free it is. A number of mulches, such as peat moss and pine needles are acidic, making them an excellent mulch for rhododendrons and azaleas but for few other plants.

USING MULCH

First Lay down a plastic weed barrier before mulching.

Next Transport mulch to area and apply over weed barrier.

Last Rake mulch around plants making sure that mulch does not touch stems of shrubs.

40

Composting

Compost can be made by collecting waste materials from your home and yard—grass clippings, shredded leaves, spent flowers and kitchen vegetable waste. All you need to create this rich soil conditioner is an area in which to collect this material, let it break down for several months, turning occasionally, and adding soil and water. You can either build your own compost bin, or select one from an increasingly wide variety available at garden centers and nurseries.

What to Put into the Compost Pile

- Grass clippings
- Leaves, whole and shredded
- Kitchen vegetable waste—coffee grounds, tea leaves, fruit and vegetable rinds, parings, eggshells, etc.
- Manure—horse, cow, goat, or poultry
- Garden wastes—spent flower stalks or heads, vegetable tops, corn stalks, etc.
- Seaweed or kelp

What *Not* to Put into the Compost Pile

- Meat or fish scraps (attracts animals)
- Pet manures (may contain disease)
- Grass clippings or other plants that have been treated with weed killer or other harmful chemicals
- Diseased plants
- Weeds that may have seeds or viable roots

WHEN NOT TO MULCH

Although mulch is one of the most useful tools to the gardener, there are some potential disadvantages to mulching.

Seedlings Soil into which seed has been sown directly should not be mulched. Because this soil must be consistently moist, the mulch will keep the soil at a high humidity creating perfect conditions for damping-off disease, a fungus that causes seedlings to rot at the base of the soil and fall over and die. Seedlings must be established and a minimum of three to four inches high before you lay down a mulch. Keep mulch away from the stem or base to ensure good air circulation.

Perennials Prone to Crown Rot Crown rot affects a number of perennials and is a disease caused by a fungus that favors damp or rainy conditions. Avoid mulching after heavy rains when soil is waterlogged. Keep mulch three to four inches away from the stem of foxglove and other plants the crown rot may affect.

There are other disadvantages to mulching, but they are small in comparison to the benefits. Soil will not warm up quickly enough in the spring if mulches are applied too early. Tomatoes and corn need warm soil and their growth can be delayed if mulch is applied prematurely. Some mulches, such as sawdust, wood chips and straw, can cause nitrogen depletion as they decompose. This is easily corrected by using additional nitrogen as a fertilizer. And, occasionally, mulches provide a home for mice and slugs.

THE RIGHT PLANT FOR THE RIGHT AREA

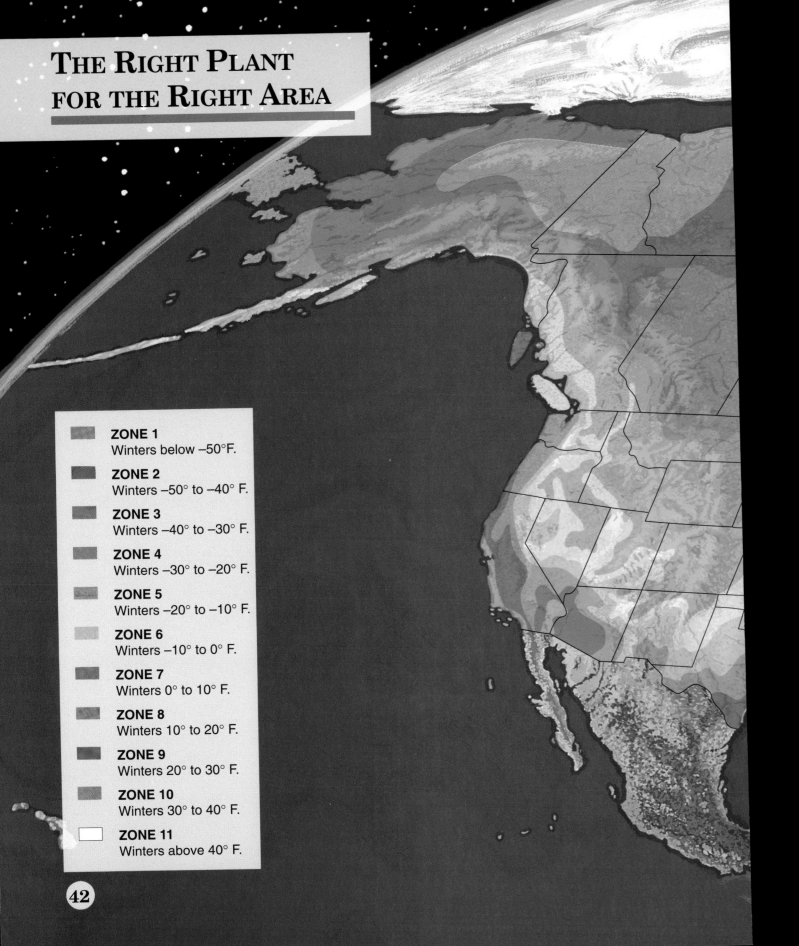

ZONE 1
Winters below −50°F.

ZONE 2
Winters −50° to −40° F.

ZONE 3
Winters −40° to −30° F.

ZONE 4
Winters −30° to −20° F.

ZONE 5
Winters −20° to −10° F.

ZONE 6
Winters −10° to 0° F.

ZONE 7
Winters 0° to 10° F.

ZONE 8
Winters 10° to 20° F.

ZONE 9
Winters 20° to 30° F.

ZONE 10
Winters 30° to 40° F.

ZONE 11
Winters above 40° F.

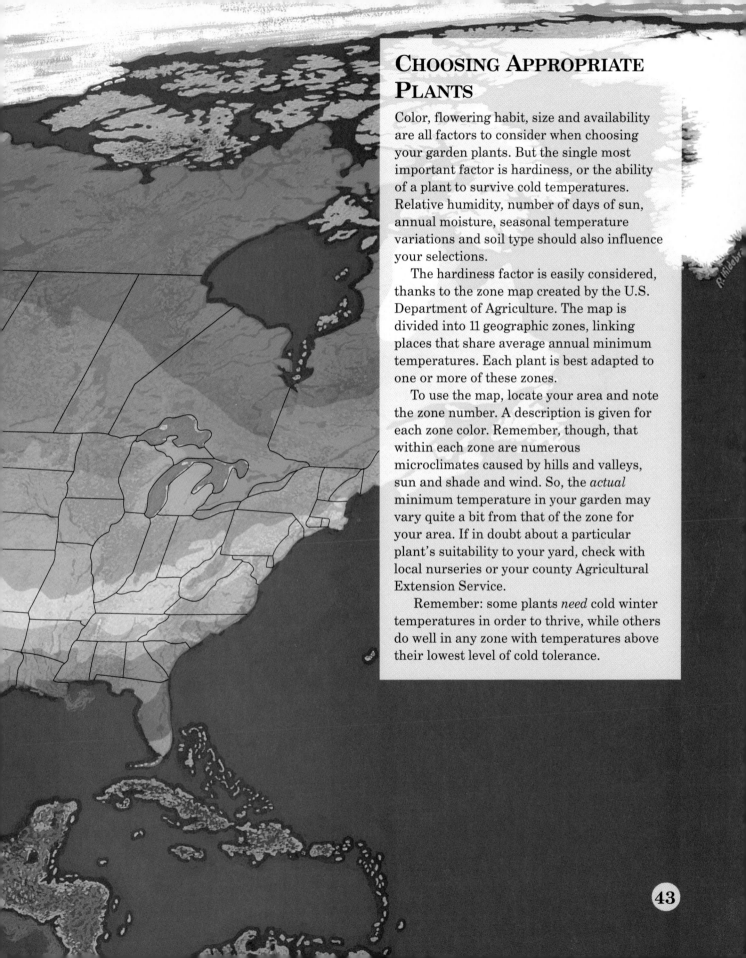

CHOOSING APPROPRIATE PLANTS

Color, flowering habit, size and availability are all factors to consider when choosing your garden plants. But the single most important factor is hardiness, or the ability of a plant to survive cold temperatures. Relative humidity, number of days of sun, annual moisture, seasonal temperature variations and soil type should also influence your selections.

The hardiness factor is easily considered, thanks to the zone map created by the U.S. Department of Agriculture. The map is divided into 11 geographic zones, linking places that share average annual minimum temperatures. Each plant is best adapted to one or more of these zones.

To use the map, locate your area and note the zone number. A description is given for each zone color. Remember, though, that within each zone are numerous microclimates caused by hills and valleys, sun and shade and wind. So, the *actual* minimum temperature in your garden may vary quite a bit from that of the zone for your area. If in doubt about a particular plant's suitability to your yard, check with local nurseries or your county Agricultural Extension Service.

Remember: some plants *need* cold winter temperatures in order to thrive, while others do well in any zone with temperatures above their lowest level of cold tolerance.

LOW-MAINTENANCE LAWNS

CHOOSING GRASS FOR MINIMAL CARE

Before starting a low-maintenance lawn, determine if your lawn can be renovated or if you should remove it and start over. Renovation is easier and less expensive. Examine your lawn carefully. If more than 50–60 percent of the lawn is weed-ridden, diseased and in generally poor condition, reconstruction is necessary.

Choosing the right grass is critical to reducing maintenance. If you are establishing a new lawn, be sure and select a grass that is right for your climatic conditions, soil type and your life-style. Do not choose a grass that requires a lot of watering or fertilizing.

Check around before purchasing grass seed. Ask your local nursery for advice on low-maintenance lawn grass.

Lawn grasses are classified as cool-season and warm-season grasses. For cool-season grasses, fescues and improved perennial ryegrass are both relatively low maintenance; warm-season grasses include zoysia, Bermudagrass or centipedegrass. Look for improved varieties, such as Mid-South turf-type tall fescues—these are bred to be disease, heat or drought resistant, depending on the variety. Mixes of several kinds of seed improve disease resistance and can produce a lawn that does well in sun or shade. For deep shade, under low-branching trees or where there are surface roots, plant a groundcover. No grass will grow well under these conditions.

RETHINKING LAWN AREAS

More than likely the most high-maintenance area of your property is the lawn. It requires mowing, weeding, watering, fertilizing, edging, raking and possibly reseeding or dethatching, and some of these chores are needed on a weekly basis.

Despite the amount of work it requires, a lawn is important when there are children and pets to consider, or when family activities include lawn sports. Remember that simple geometric shapes such as a square or a rectangle are easier to maintain than intricately curved or scalloped edges.

To decrease maintenance, reduce the size of your lawn by replacing large sections with shrubs or flower borders or an expanse of groundcovers. The result will be a smaller, contained lawn that still retains the beauty of a large expanse of green grass. You can also create large deck or pavement areas in the back yard. Whatever you choose, adjust the size of your lawn to suit your needs and do not leave it any larger than you can care for.

Edge the lawn with mowing strips so you can easily maintain its boundary. Bricks make an especially attractive mowing strip, but you can also use paving, lawn edging or railroad ties. Design the lawn so that it does not grow right up to trees. This will eliminate the time-consuming task of clipping around the trunks.

Another possibility is to turn part or all of your lawn into a meadow. Meadow or wildflower areas are easy to establish and usually include native plants that provide a variety of textures and colors. You need only prepare the soil and sow a wildflower seed mixture. Wildflowers require minimum maintenance but can be a bit untidy when flowers are not in bloom (see pgs. 70–71).

GROUNDCOVERS

GROUNDCOVERS REDUCE MAINTENANCE

Groundcovers can reduce or even replace a lawn. They are neat, attractive and require substantially less maintenance than lawn grass. If you want to reduce your workload, consider mass planting one or a variety of groundcovers.

A combination of lawn and groundcovers works well. Alternating graceful curves of groundcovers around trees and the foundation of the house provides texture, variety and visual interest. Most groundcovers are low-growing, need very little pruning and many are evergreen.

Groundcovers often grow well where lawns don't. Planting and mowing grass on slopes is difficult; groundcovers will set roots firmly and keep erosion in check. Shaded areas under low-branching trees will be unable to sustain grass growth; ivy, pachysandra or wild ginger will thrive.

Groundcovers also do well in areas that are too wet or too dry for lawn grasses. A low area in the shade that may not drain well is perfect for a mass planting of feathery ferns; a hot, dry area above a retaining wall that is difficult and dangerous to mow is ideal for ivy or snow-in-summer.

Groundcovers require very little grooming other than occasional trimming or fertilizing; they are readily planted and enjoyed.

Ivy
Hedera species
A ground-hugging vine with dark green, evergreen leaves. Easy to establish, grows 10–12 in. high; excellent for shade in dry areas. Will climb trees, fences or walls.

Periwinkle
Vinca minor
Hardy, evergreen leaves with pretty blue flowers in the spring; Tough and long-lasting, grows to 6–8 in.; does well in deep shade.

Snow-in-Summer
Cerastium tomentosum
A fast-growing perennial that forms a mat of white, woolly, 1 in. green-gray leaves. Grows to 6 in. with 1-in. white flowers that appear in spring and early summer. Does well in sun and hot weather.

Spotted Dead Nettle
Lamium maculatum 'Beacon Silver'
A colorful perennial with pink flowers in the spring atop unusual silver foliage with narrow green edgings. Grows 6–8 in. in shade or part shade.

Japanese Spurge
Pachysandra terminalis
Most widely used of all groundcovers. Moderate-growth; foliage is evergreen, 5–10 in. high. Thrives in deep shade.

Hosta
Hosta species
Mounding, slow growth to 3 ft. Comes in a variety of sizes and foliage shapes with many color variations of green to yellow to variegated. Spike-like lavender or white flowers in late summer. Part sun to deep shade, moist soil.

Moss Phlox
Phlox subulata
Matting perennial with semi-evergreen, needle-like foliage to 6 in. Pink, purple flowers in spring. Sun, well-drained soil.

Wild Ginger
Asarum europaeum
Moderate-growing evergreen with glossy 2–3 in. diameter leaves. Grows 6–8 in. high; Excellent shade plant.

LOW-MAINTENANCE TREES

LOW-CARE TREES

Trees provide shade, texture and color. Planting low-maintenance trees requires careful consideration. Choose trees that are slow growing, need little pruning, are relatively free from disease and insects and can grow in average soils. Trees that fit these criteria will need a minimum of trimming, spraying and other tasks.

Select new trees for shade, flowers, fruit or ornamental beauty. Keep in mind that they should be in scale with their surroundings, and should not drop messy fruit or shed bark, like the sycamore. Avoid trees known for serious disease or insect problems such as elms, and trees that are short-lived such as poplars and mimosa.

Choose trees with more than one season of interest. If you need a large tree to shade the house, look for one that flowers in the spring or produces a gorgeous display of color in the fall. Flowering, non-fruiting trees can add interest, while the large shade trees provide fall color.

Shade trees provide beauty as well as cool shade. Select varieties that do not become brittle and lose branches in storms and do not disperse seedlings. Many improved seedless trees are available.

Specimen trees are simply trees that are either attractive or interesting enough, usually throughout the year, to merit being singled out for a special position. Sometimes this is for color, a striking form or spectacular and unusual leaf shape. The Japanese maple and White Fringe tree are examples.

White Fringe Tree
Chionanthus species
White, airy, fragrant flowers in late spring and yellow fall color; grows 15–25 ft; sun, moist soil; Zones 5–9.

Japanese Maple
Acer palmatum
A small tree with excellent fall color that grows to 20 ft. Ornamental with a graceful habit; full sun to part shade, moist soil. Zones 5–9.

Flowering Cherry
Prunus species
Ornamental tree with stunning floral display in the spring; beautiful bark in the winter. Grows to 20 ft. Full sun, moist soil. Zones 5–9.

Crabapple
Malus species
Small, rounded ornamental tree that grows to 25 ft. Pink, red or white spring blossoms, fall fruit. Zones 4–9.

Arborvitae
Thuja occidentalis
Narrow upright evergreen, grows to 60 ft. Makes a fine hedge or screen. Full sun. Tolerates wet soil. Zones 2–7.

Scotch Pine
Pinus sylvestris
This evergreen grows to 75 ft. with twisted, bluish green needles. Not dense, but open and picturesque. Full sun. Zones 2–10.

Dwarf White Spruce
Picea glauca 'Conica'
Compact pyramidal evergreen. Slow growing to 10 ft. Short fine needles soft to the touch. Zones 3–6.

Dogwood
Cornus kousa
Small flowering ornamental tree, growing to 30 ft. Blossoms are white in late spring, with fruit and scarlet foliage in fall. Zones 4–9.

Hornbeam
Carpinus betulus
Slow-growing from 30–50 ft. tall and relatively narrow. Excellent shade tree with yellow and orange color in the fall. Average soil, full sun. Zones 5–9.

49

EASY SHRUBS

EASY SHRUBS FOR LOW MAINTENANCE

Shrubs, for the most part, are easy to grow. Most require little care outside of planting them correctly. Many need little or no pruning and fertilization. And most thrive and produce abundant foliage and blooms.

Shrubs are woody plants that usually grow under 15 feet in height. They come in a wide variety of heights, shapes, foliage colors, foliage textures and forms, flower colors and forms and fruit colors.

Essential to the landscape, shrubs perform beautifully in a variety of areas—foundation plantings, borders, along walks and as a screen. A shrub border or hedge can enclose your property, providing privacy; foundation plantings can complement your house and provide a transition between the structure and the yard. Shrubs in the border can reduce maintenance while providing a background for bulbs, annuals and perennials.

When choosing shrubs for foundation planting, select varieties that are dwarf or low-growing. These will need little maintenance and won't grow and cover windows. The shrub border is a good place for beautiful flowering shrubs—let them grow naturally and allow plenty of room for them, depending on the species.

Hedges can be formal—sheared or informal—unsheared. Informal hedges are much less work than their formal counterparts. Hedge plants should be set fairly close together so they fill in densely.

Dwarf Japanese Holly
Ilex crenata 'Convexa'
Slow-growing, to 4–6 ft. Broadleaf evergreen with glossy leaves. Full sun or shade, moist soil. Zones 6–9.

Hydrangea
Hydrangea species
Grows to 5 ft. with large green leaves and masses of flowers in summer. Full to part sun, moist soil. Zones 5–10.

Mock Orange
Philadelphus hybrid
Hardy deciduous flowering shrub, grows to 10 ft. Fragrant white flowers. Full sun, average soil. Zones 4–9.

Abelia
Abelia grandiflora
Grows to 5 ft. or more. Deciduous in northern areas. Sun or part shade, well-drained soil. Zones 5–10.

Viburnum
Viburnum plicatum tomentosum
Broad-leaved evergreen or deciduous shrub from 8–12 ft. tall. Spring flowering, with red berries in the fall. Zones 4–9.

Dwarf Hinoki Cypress
Chamaecyparis obtusa cultivars
Slow-growing evergreen, needs some pruning to keep under 5 ft. Interesting spreading branch forms. Zones 5–10.

Dwarf Barberry
Berberis thunbergii 'Crimson Pigmy'
Slow-growing deciduous shrub; dense, dark red leaves, yellow flowers. Scarlet foliage, red berries in the fall. Sun to part shade; well-drained soil. Zones 4–9.

Rhododendron/Azalea
Rhododendron species
Deciduous or evergreen shrubs in a variety of sizes and shapes. Spring or summer flowering. Full or part shade in acid soil; must be kept moist. Zones 3–9.

INSTALLING TREES AND SHRUBS

MINIMIZING CARE

Most garden centers and nurseries offer trees and shrubs in three ways: bare-root, balled and burlapped or in containers.

Balled and burlapped shrubs and those in containers are easy to handle and can be planted at any time during the growing season. Less expensive, bare-root plants are dormant and the preferred form for many mail-order nurseries. Because plants are dormant, they are best planted in the early spring or late winter. Do not purchase bare-root plants that are in leaf.

Although a tree or shrub can remain balled and burlapped or in a container for a period of time, it should be planted as soon as possible. You'll be able to plant many of the small and medium-sized plants yourself. Larger trees are best left to the professional.

The preparation for planting trees and shrubs is easy. Use a slow-release fertilizer, and you will not need to refertilize for months. After the plant is in place, spread additional slow-release fertilizer around the plant and water it.

Once your trees and shrubs are in the ground, mulch heavily around the plants to three to four inches deep. Keep mulch from directly touching the trunk to allow for adequate root aeration.

A young, large tree needs staking. Tie the plant to stakes with pieces of cloth or wire, using some protection between the wire and the tree. It will take up to two years for a transplanted tree to become established, less for shrubs.

Some young trees and shrubs will need shaping. The safest time to prune is in winter when the plants are dormant; for flowering shrubs, just after bloom.

Container Plantings

First Moisten rootball and drain. Lay tree on side, loosen rootball with trowel. Remove nursery stakes. Slide container from ball. Avoid pulling trunk.

Next Cut any circling roots with knife. Dig a hole as deep as the rootball and twice as wide.

Last Set plant in hole with soil line on trunk at ground level. Fill hole with amended soil and build water basin at diameter of rootball. Water well. Stake and tie tree; remove supports after first year.

Balled and Burlapped Plantings

First Dig hole as deep as the rootball and twice as wide. Mix amendments with soil from hole.

Next Place plant in hole with burlap. Remove string. Loosen and pull down sides of burlap, leaving the bottom in place. Trim any circling roots.

Last Fill hole with amended soil and build water basin at diameter of rootball. Water well. Stake and tie; remove supports after first year.

Low-Maintenance Perennials

Daylilies
Hemerocallis hybrids
Striking trumpets of brightly colored, multiple flowers on stalks 8–48 in. Full or part sun, average soil. Zones 3–9.

Choosing Low-Maintenance Perennials

Perennials are plants that bloom year after year. They grow from the rootstock, the top of the plant dying after its bloom season and the root remaining alive to send up new growth each spring. Perennials are a reliable source of flowers for the low-maintenance gardener; once planted, many need very little care. The only disadvantage to perennials is their brief blooming season.

For low-maintenance landscapes, keep flower beds small. Or, at least, start small until you know the extent of maintenance you are willing to do. Design, layout and choice of the lowest care perennials will ensure low-maintenance flower beds.

When selecting perennials, avoid plants that need frequent dividing, thinning, pruning or deadheading. Choose instead those that are long-lived and rarely need dividing, for example, peonies, Oriental poppies, wild blue indigo and daylilies.

In addition to flowers, some provide handsome foliage and interesting texture, such as ferns and hosta. There are a number of perennials that remain evergreen in warmer parts of the country, such as lilyturf, barrenwort, Christmas rose and agapanthus.

Shasta Daisy
Chrysanthemum maximum
A sunny garden classic whose flowers have white, radiating petals from a bright yellow center. Grows up to 4 ft. in average soils. Sun to part shade. Zones 5–9.

Agapanthus
Agapanthus species
Fountain-like clumps with tall stems of sky blue or white flowers. Grows 18–48 in. in sun to part shade. Drought tolerant after established. Zones 9–10.

Peony
Paeonia lactiflora
Single or double flowers up to 4 in. wide; bloom in whites, pinks and reds in late spring, summer. Bushy plants up to 3 ft. Sun or part shade, rich soil. Zones 2–8.

Hens and Chicks
Sempervivum species
A hardy, popular plant. Sturdy rosettes of grayish leaves with pink flowers. Grows to 6 in. Tolerates poor and sandy soil. Full sun. Zones 4–10.

Stonecrop
Sedum spectabile
Showy clusters of tiny pink flowers above succulent green leaves. Grows 18–24 in. in full sun. Tolerates dry soil. Zones 3–10.

Gas Plant
Dictamnus albus
Sturdy, long-lived clumps with white or pink flowers on 30–48 in. spikes in summer. Sun or part shade in good soil. Seldom needs dividing. Zones 3–5.

Blanketflower
Gaillardia grandiflora
One of the longest blooming perennial flowers—from June through October—with red or yellow flowers. Grows 12–30 in. Full sun. Tolerates poor soils. Zones 3–9.

CAREFREE BULBS

WORK-FREE COLOR

Bulbs provide spectacular beauty in a rainbow of colors from late winter all the way through the fall. Dependable bloomers, bulbs return year after year and require very little care. In fact, once you plant a bulb, most of the work is done. All you need to do is fertilize once a year and water periodically.

The first blooms of early spring bulbs are a welcome sight after a long winter. Crocuses, glory-of-the-snow and snowdrops are the first to appear, followed by daffodils, hyacinths, bluebells and tulips. There are a number of bulbs, such as lilies, cannas, crocosmias and gladiola that supply color all summer. And for the fall, there are alliums and fall-blooming crocuses. With a proper selection of bulbs, you can enjoy a succession of bloom throughout the entire growing season. To ensure flowers year after year, be sure to snip off spent ones.

For the lowest maintenance garden, choose bulbs that are easy to grow in your soil and climate. Take note of which ones grow in your neighborhood or ask at the nursery. Plant only hardy bulbs that can stay in the ground all winter. Tender bulbs, like gladiolus, dahlias and cannas need to be dug out and stored each fall. However, if you live in an area where the ground doesn't freeze, these bulbs can remain once planted.

Many flowers are referred to as bulbs but are actually tubers, corms or rhizomes. For example, iris is a rhizome, but functions much like a bulb.

Windflower
Anemone blanda
Grows up to 8 in. and hugs the ground with white, pink, purple or blue flowers. Very hardy, grows in any well-drained soil. Sun or part shade. Zones 5–9.

Snowdrop
Galanthus nivalis
Blooms late winter and early spring with white, nodding flowers. Grows 4–6 in. in full sun or part shade in well-drained soil. Zones 3–7.

Grape Hyacinth
Muscari species
Small flower spikes of blue bloom in early spring.
Excellent for massing. Grows 8–12 in.; sun to part
shade, well-drained soil. Zones 3–10.

Daffodil
Narcissus species and hybrids
Spring-flowering bulb that has a trumpet-shaped flower
and comes in yellow, white, pink, orange, green and
bicolor. Sun to part shade, well-drained soil. Zones 4–10.

Tulip
Tulipa gregii
The best work-free species are *T. gregii*, *T. kaufmanniana*
or hybrids of these. All are smaller than the common tulip,
but do not need the usual replanting and come in many
colors. Full sun, well-drained soil. Zones 2–9.

Crocus
Crocus species
Early spring or fall flowering with blossoms of purple,
white or yellow. Grows 6–8 in. in full sun or shade.
Excellent in masses. Well-drained soil. Zones 3–9.

PLANTING AND CARING FOR PERENNIALS AND BULBS

Planting Bulbs

First Dig a hole 6–12 in. deep, depending upon garden soil and bulb type. Amend soil and fertilize with bone meal.

Last Place bulb in hole, points up and knob side down; space bulbs 4–6 in. apart. Cover with soil and water thoroughly.

Planting Perennials

First Dig holes twice as wide and as deep as roots, loosen soil and mix with organic compost and all-purpose fertilizer.

Next Remove plants from container, pushing from bottom. Cut any encircling roots, loosen rootball. Place plant in hole, position to ground level.

Last Fill with improved soil, firm soil around plant. Water well, reposition plants if necessary.

CARING FOR BULBS AND PERENNIALS

Plant your bulb garden in areas of full sun or light shade. You can arrange your spring-blooming bulbs under deciduous trees that aren't in full leaf until summer. Make sure there is adequate drainage before planting; bulbs do poorly in soggy soil. A deep, well-prepared soil bed will greatly increase the life of your bulbs. Add bone meal or superphosphate at planting time and set them at the proper depth—approximately three times the diameter of the bulb—for long-lasting beauty.

Hardy bulbs do not perform the same in all areas. In the warmer Zones 9 and 10, hardy tulips and snowdrops often perform poorly because they do not get the chill necessary to break dormancy. In these areas, dig up the bulbs and store them in the refrigerator for six to eight weeks; replant in mid-winter.

Spring-blooming bulbs should be planted in the fall. Summer-flowering bulbs should be planted in the spring after the last frost.

Because perennials will remain in place for several years, it is essential to prepare the soil before planting. Prepare the bed at least ten to 12 inches deep with plenty of humus, and make sure the soil is well drained. Use mulch to keep weeds in check and pull any by hand that may poke through. Water during dry spells and cultivate 5–10–5 fertilizer into the soil surface.

For successive color all through the season, plant mixed borders of bulbs, perennials and annuals.

ANNUALS FOR EASY COLOR

EASY SPOTS OF COLOR

Annuals are plants which complete their life cycle within the space of one year. Annuals germinate from a seed, grow into mature plants, flower, set seed and die. They are easy to grow and flourish in most kinds of climates.

Although annuals must be planted each year, they produce abundant blossoms of nonstop color for months. Most begin blooming early in the season and flower until frost, supplying the summer garden with continuous color, while perennials and shrubs may bloom only briefly.

Annuals can be started by seed or purchased as young plants. Either form is relatively inexpensive. Start seeds indoors in mid to late winter in order to have transplants large enough to set outdoors after danger of frost. If you choose to purchase plants, do so in late spring or early summer (fall and winter for the warmer regions).

Annuals are classified as hardy, half-hardy and tender. Hardy annuals can withstand light frost, and seeds can be sown as soon as the soil is workable. Half-hardy annuals will tolerate short periods of cold, but several frosts can kill them; sow these seeds after danger of frost has passed. Tender annuals will not survive any frost, and seeds can only be sown when the soil has warmed.

When selecting annuals for low maintenance, choose those that do not need staking—these require more care and tending. Look for plants that do not need deadheading (removing of fading flowers), or limit the amount of annuals that need deadheading to keep this task to a minimum. Many annuals readily reseed themselves and never need replanting after the first year.

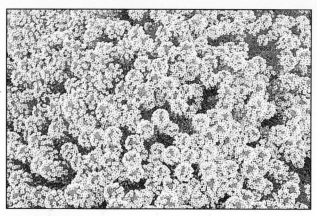

Sweet Alyssum
Lobularia maritima
Low-growing plants of 4–6 in. with tiny clusters of fragrant white, pink or purple flowers. Excellent edging plant. Sun or part shade. Reseeds.

Cosmos
Cosmos species
Tall annual, growing 4–6 ft. with delicate foliage and blooms of pink, red, white. Small varieties are 1–3 ft. in orange and yellow. Full sun, dry soil. Reseeds.

Begonia
Begonia x *semperflorens*
Continuous display of small flowers in pink, white and red. Excellent for beds, border or containers. Grows 6–12 in. Sun or part shade. Blooms year round in Zones 9–10.

Cleome
Cleome species
A dramatic, tall plant with large pink and white flower heads and long spider-like stamens. Grows 3–6 ft. in sun or light shade. Does not need deadheading.

Impatiens
Impatiens wallerana
Brilliant, nonstop blooms for shady areas in many colors. Easy to grow in cool, moist soil. Shade and part shade. Available in a full color spectrum.

Lobelia
Lobelia erinus
Low-growing and trailing plants in vivid purples and blues. Excellent for edging and shade. Sun or part shade, moist soil. Grows 4–8 in. Reseeds.

Zinnia
Zinnia elegans
Popular annual, grows to 2–3 ft. with large, 2–6 in. flowers in all colors. Full sun. Rich, well-drained soil.

Marigold
Tagetes species
Sturdy, long-flowering annual with bright yellow, orange, and red-brown flowers. Wide variety from 8–36 in. tall. Full sun, well-drained soil.

PLANTING AND CARING FOR ANNUALS

Annuals require more care than trees or shrubs but reward you with colorful blooms all season. If chosen wisely and mulched to conserve water and control weeding, annuals will need only minimal maintenance.

Pinching Back

Pinching back new growth will force stems to branch, creating bushier, more compact plants. Pinch off the top point of the stem above mature leaves.

Deadheading

Deadheading, or cutting off faded blossoms, will stop seed production and thereby promote more flowering. It also keeps the plant tidy and attractive.

Transplanting Annuals

First Prepare the bed in advance, adding fertilizer and amendments. Remove plant from container by pressing on the sides and bottom.

Next Use a trowel to dig a hole large enough to accommodate the rootball.

Last Press soil firmly around plant and water.

CARE OF ANNUALS

Preparing your soil properly will ensure the growth of healthy plants. Annuals are shallow-rooted, and therefore preparation can be less extensive than for perennials. They can be grown in some locations where topsoil is not deep nor drainage good enough for perennials.

Most annuals need a sunny location and rich, well-drained soil. Add plenty of compost and an all-purpose fertilizer to your bed or border. Choose annuals that are suitable to your climate—many need consistent moisture while others are heat or drought tolerant. Planting those which best suit your conditions will ensure steady growth and vigorous plants and also minimize your workload.

If choosing plants from a nursery, be sure to purchase carefully. Buy plants that are a healthy green color with no pests; they should be bushy and compact with only a few blooms; roots should not be coming out of the drainage holes. Look for clearly labeled plants that are disease and pest resistant.

Annuals are perfect for relatively work-free pots and hanging baskets. Simply fill the container with potting soil—not soil from the garden which may contain weeds or pests—and add slow-release fertilizer. After your plants are in, you need only keep the container watered.

VEGETABLE GARDENS

GROW GREAT VEGETABLES WITH MINIMUM WORK

No matter how small the garden, there should always be room for vegetables. Many people deprive themselves of this pleasure because they think they do not have enough space; or that growing vegetables is too time-consuming. With proper planning and the use of efficiency methods you can have a vegetable garden with high yields from low maintenance. The key is taking advantage of three gardening techniques: intensive planting, interplanting and succession planting.

Intensive planting is geared to yield the greatest possible harvest in small places. The key is to create rich, fertile soil and to space plants closely and intermittently rather than in rows. The result is more efficient, allowing for more plants and, thus, higher yields. Intensive planting in areas defined by blocks is known as *square foot gardening*.

Interplanting puts two compatible crops in an area normally planted with only one. When one is harvested, the other has room to grow, making efficient use of space.

The main thrust of succession planting is to plant the same vegetable at different times for continuous and long harvests. You can plant in two to three week intervals or plant early-, mid- and late-season cultivars, thus creating successive harvest dates.

Using any or all of these methods will reduce work and produce high yields in small spaces.

PLANTING TIPS

All vegetable gardens take work, but there are a number of things you can do to reduce time and labor.

- Select disease-resistant cultivars.
- Rotate crops each year to avoid disease and pests, if you have the space.
- Choose low-maintenance and high-yield vegetables.
- Maximize garden space and increase productivity by growing vine crops on vertical supports.
- Make successive plantings of the same vegetable in 2–3 week intervals to prolong harvest.
- Use intensive gardening techniques to reduce work and increase yields.
- Mulch, mulch, mulch. This will save lots of time weeding and watering.
- Make use of interplant cropping .
- Grow your vegetables in raised beds where you can control the soil mix and irrigation.
- Grow looseleaf lettuces instead of head types. They are quicker and easier to grow.
- Plant corn in blocks, not rows, for best pollination.
- Plants that do well in part shade are the leaf crops—lettuce, spinach, chard, mustard greens and parsley.

Easy Vegetables to Grow

Beans	Onions
Beets	Peas
Cabbage	Peppers
Carrots	Radishes
Corn	Spinach
Cucumbers	Tomatoes
Kale	Zucchini
Lettuce	

BUILDING RAISED-BED GARDENS

SAVING TIME AND ENERGY

Raised beds are favored by gardeners whose garden soil is poor or otherwise unworkable. But raised beds offer advantages well beyond improving soil conditions. Raised beds provide efficient, easily tended and well-defined planting space for the low-maintenance gardener.

Raised beds can be any size or shape but should be at east 10–12 in. deep for deep-rooted crops like carrots or turnips. A depth of 6–8 in. is sufficient for other crops as long as the soil beneath the raised bed is penetrable. The recommended method for preparing the soil is digging 12–18 in. and adding lots of organic matter. This will ensure a loose, deep, fertile soil that water and roots penetrate easily. Raised beds are framed in wood and usually are four feet wide so that crops can be reached easily from the sides.

Advantages of Raised-Bed Gardening:

- Wet or low-lying areas can be productive since bed allows water to drain from soil.

- Soil warms up more quickly, enabling quicker planting and harvesting.

- Once soil is prepared, it remains protected, and cultivating and digging are kept to a minimum. Amended soil is not wasted in pathways.

- A compact growing area means less—and easier—watering and labor.

- Raised beds allow for deep, healthy root systems, which also help plants cope better with drought.

- Yield per square foot of growing space is higher than in traditional rows.

Materials

String, stakes for marking (or use garden lime)

Spade or shovel

Garden tiller (optional)

Wheelbarrow

2 x 12 untreated redwood or cedar lumber (linear feet of bed perimeter)

1 x 3 x 2 ft. untreated redwood or cedar stakes (2 per corner plus 1 every 16 in.)

1/4 x 3-in. lag screws (2 per stake plus 3 per corner)

◆ **CAUTION**

Never use pressure-treated lumber for vegetables.

Raised-Bed Planter

First Choose and mark site. Remove any weeds or turf.

Then Till or turn over soil. Dig shallow trench along border.

Next Fasten edge boards to stakes with lag screws. Bottom is 2 in. under soil surface.

Last Fill bed with soil, add amendments and fertilizer. Mix thoroughly and rake.

ORNAMENTAL GRASSES

USING DECORATIVE GRASSES

Ornamental grasses are versatile, adaptable and are increasingly popular in today's landscapes. They come in all shapes and sizes from low growing to tall, graceful fountain-like forms that are quite stunning. In addition to their visual appeal, ornamental grasses generally require little maintenance. Most do not need deadheading, staking or spraying and grow in a variety of climates and conditions. Many even have year-round appeal.

Decorative and ornamental grasses add a new and varied element to the landscape. Grasses can be used alone, in groupings, in combination with other grasses or as complements to perennials and shrubs. Some can be used as groundcovers or as a special accent plant. Foliage may be green, yellow, gray, blue-green, reddish brown or variegated. Many have beautiful golden and orange-rust colors in the fall. Several have feathery plumes or small clusters of flowers. All are interesting and add an unusual touch to the landscape.

Plant ornamental grasses in the spring for best results. This is also the time to cut back the deciduous species when new growth is starting. Shear to 4–6 in. Propagation and division is also best done in the early spring.

The adaptability and variety of ornamental grasses make them useful for a number of environments from the seashore to the bog garden.

Bloodgrass
Imperata cylindrica 'Rubra'
Brilliant green and red foliage that lasts throughout the growing season. Slow-growing, spreads by rhizomes. Grows 1–2 ft. Sun, part shade, well-drained soil. Zones 6–10.

Eulaliagrass
Miscanthus sinensis
A tall, graceful clumping grass with slender leaves. Silky flower spikes appear an 6–8 in. stems in fall. Moist soil. Zones 6–9.

Feather Reedgrass
Calamagrostis x *acutiflora* 'Stricta'
Tall hybrid reedgrass with rigidly erect stems to 5 ft. Full sun or part shade, damp soil. Zones 5–10.

Blue Oatgrass
Helictotrichon sempervirens
Blue-gray clumping grass, grows to 3–4 ft. Needs full sun or light shade, well-drained soil. Zones 4–10.

Variegated Sedge
Carex morrowii 'Aureo-Variegata'
Clump-forming sedge growing 1–1 1/2 ft, with bright yellow grass-like blades with green edges. Full sun to part shade in rich, moist soil. Zones 5–9.

Giant Feathergrass
Stipa gigantea
Fine-stemmed feather grass with golden plumes grows up to 6 ft. tall. Full sun, well-drained soil. Zones 5–10.

Zebragrass
Miscanthus sinensis 'Zebrinus'
A tall, bright green grass with creamy yellow bands running across the leaves. Flower spikes appear in fall. Prefers a moist soil. Zones 6–9.

Blue Fescue
Festuca ovina glauca
Mounds of silvery-blue leaves to 12 in. Good for borders, accents or groundcovers. Full sun and light, well-drained soil. Zones 4–10.

69

WILDFLOWER AND MEADOW GARDENS

GARDENING WITH WILDFLOWERS

Wildflowers are usually defined as flowering plants that grow without intentional cultivation or the aid of people. Most wildflowers are species native to our country, but many introduced plants have also naturalized and become commonplace.

Woodland wildflowers are more exacting about their environmental conditions and are, thus, more labor-intensive than meadow varieties. Meadow, prairie and grassland wildflowers usually reseed themselves readily and grow quickly, making them easy to establish and maintain.

Most meadow wildflowers and grasses occur naturally in treeless fields with well-drained soil. Most are easily grown from seed and transplanted; ready-made mixtures are available. They should be grown in open and sunny areas. Ordinary garden soil is fine. In fact, most wildflowers actually thrive in dry, poor soil and can withstand drought. Allow room for them to reseed themselves and form natural drifts.

Wildflower meadows make an excellent and striking alternative to grass and require much less maintenance than lawns. But before you turn your front lawn into a wildflower area, check local ordinances to see if mowing is a requirement. Neighbors have been known to call the authorities.

WILDFLOWER MIXTURES

By choosing the individual plants for your wildflower meadow, you can create color groupings for more visual appeal, and you can distinguish your seedlings from the weeds. If you don't have the time or can't wait to select your own, there is an alternative: purchasing a premixed wildflower formula. But, take care. Choosing a mixture can be very confusing.

Read the flower mixture label carefully. The more specific the mixture is, the better the results. Choose a seed mixture for your particular region of the country, and only purchase a mix if it lists the proportions of each type of seed. Be wary of the amount of grass seed and potentially invasive species included in the mix. Lawn grass seed is inexpensive and often used as filler. Avoid mixtures with annual ryegrass, orchardgrass, Timothy grass and bluegrass.

Mixtures do have the advantage of many different kinds of flowers, some of which will be new to you. One of the main problems with mixtures, however, is that desirable species are often left out because they are expensive or difficult to collect. Aster and goldenrod are two that fall into this category, and both provide excellent fall color. Purchase these separately to include in the wildflower meadow.

Wildflower meadows will require annual care. Despite what many think, you cannot purchase a wildflower mixture, scatter the seed and return to the deck chair. After spreading the seed, lightly mulch to keep the seeds from blowing away and keep moist until germination. Mixtures include annuals and perennials. The annuals will bloom the first year, perennials the second. Many of both will reseed, many will not. Replant your favorite annuals each year. After your plants are established, most are drought resistant, but water during very dry spells.

PLANTS FOR SPECIAL USES

Easy Annuals

Calendula	Marigold
Candytuft	Nasturtium
Celosia	Petunia
Cleome	Phlox
Coleus	Portulaca
Gloriosa Daisy	Salvia
Impatiens	Sweet Alyssum
Lobelia	Wax Begonia

Self-Sowing Annuals

Bachelor's Button	Nasturtium
Calendula	Nemophila
California Poppy	Nicotiana
Clarkia	Pansy
Cleome	Poppy
Cosmos	Portulaca
Lunaria	Sweet Alyssum
Morning Glory	

Low-Growing Foundation Shrubs

Azalea (dwarf and others)
Dwarf Japanese Holly
English Yew
Japanese Yew
Mugo Pine
Rhododendron P.J.M. (and others)

Shrubs for Informal Hedges or Natural Form

Azalea	Forsythia
Barberry	Privet
Bayberry	Rhododendron
Boxwood	Spirea
Euonymous	Viburnum
Fothergilla	Weigela

Low-Maintenance Bulbs

Crocus	Leucojum
Daffodil	Lily
Galanthus	Siberian Squill
Glory-of-the-Snow	Snowdrop
Grape Hyacinth	Spanish Bluebell
Iris	Windflower

Low-Maintenance Perennials

Agapanthus	Japanese Anemone
Balloon Flower	Lamb's Ear
Bergenia	Lavender
Black-Eyed Susan	Liriope
Butterfly Weed	Penstemon
Catmint	Peony
Coral Bells	Purple Cone Flower
Coreopsis	Santolina
Daylilies	Sedum
Ferns	Siberian Iris
Gay Feather	Stonecrop
Hellebore	Thrift
Heliopsis	Wild Ginger
Hens and Chicks	Yarrow
Hosta	

PLANTS FOR SHADE

Shade Annuals

Alyssum   Impatiens
Begonia   Pansy
Coleus   Torenia

Shade Perennials

Bleeding Heart   Japanese Anemone
Daylily   Lungwort
Ferns   Penstemon
Foxglove   Woodland Phlox
Hosta

Shade Groundcovers

Ajuga   Liriope
Barrenwort   Pachysandra
Bergenia   Wild Ginger
Ivy   Wintercreeper
Lamium

Shade Shrubs

Aucuba   Mountain Laurel
Azalea   Nandina
Japanese Holly   Rhododendron
Kerria   Skimmia
Leucothoe   Viburnum
Mahonia

DROUGHT-TOLERANT PLANTS

Drought-Tolerant Annuals

California Poppy   Nasturtium
Cleome   Poppy
Cosmos   Portulaca
Creeping Zinnia   Sunflower
Globe Amaranth

Drought-Tolerant Perennials

Artemesia   Lamb's Ear
Black-Eyed Susan   Purple Rock Cress
Butterfly Weed   Santolina
Centaurea   Scabiosa
Coreopsis   Sea Pink
Gaillardia   Sedum
Globe Thistle   Yarrow
Golden Marguerite

Drought-Tolerant Shrubs

Barberry   Juniper
Bayberry   Nandina
Broom   Oleander
Ceanothus   Rockrose
Chinese Holly   Rugosa Rose
Cotoneaster

Seasonal Calendar

No matter how low maintenance you make your garden, there are always some chores that will have to be done. Organize the tasks by weekly and monthly routines to fit your needs. Here is a sample calendar by season.

Spring

- Purchase seeds.
- Prepare soil as soon as it is workable.
- Purchase annuals and perennials not grown from seed.
- Fertilize shrubs, trees and perennials as growth begins.
- Fertilize lawn and water thoroughly.
- Divide and replant perennials, if needed.
- Replace and replenish mulches.
- Take any winter protection off young trees and shrubs.
- Start mowing lawn when growth begins.
- Plant summer-blooming bulbs.
- Plant vegetable garden in raised beds.
- Watch for pests.

Summer

- In late spring or early summer, plant containers, pots or hanging baskets with annuals. Fertilize with slow-release fertilizer.
- Plant annuals and summer bulbs as soon as soil warms in late spring or early summer. Fertilize with an all-purpose fertilizer. Pinch back annuals for bushier growth.
- Maintain lawn as needed.
- Prune spring-flowering trees and shrubs and vines as necessary.
- Trim dead foliage of spring flowering bulbs.
- Water plants as needed. A thorough soaking is better than several sprinklings.
- Deadhead annuals and perennials as necessary.
- Watch for pests and any sign of disease; act immediately at first sign.
- Harvest vegetables.

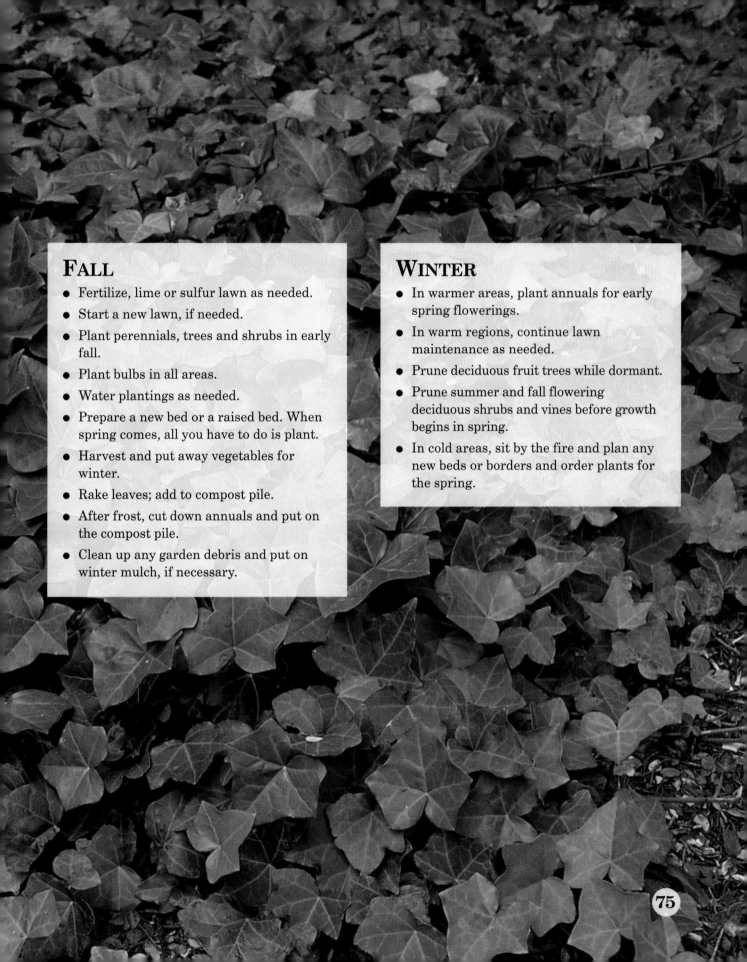

FALL

- Fertilize, lime or sulfur lawn as needed.
- Start a new lawn, if needed.
- Plant perennials, trees and shrubs in early fall.
- Plant bulbs in all areas.
- Water plantings as needed.
- Prepare a new bed or a raised bed. When spring comes, all you have to do is plant.
- Harvest and put away vegetables for winter.
- Rake leaves; add to compost pile.
- After frost, cut down annuals and put on the compost pile.
- Clean up any garden debris and put on winter mulch, if necessary.

WINTER

- In warmer areas, plant annuals for early spring flowerings.
- In warm regions, continue lawn maintenance as needed.
- Prune deciduous fruit trees while dormant.
- Prune summer and fall flowering deciduous shrubs and vines before growth begins in spring.
- In cold areas, sit by the fire and plan any new beds or borders and order plants for the spring.

TOOLS AND EQUIPMENT

TOOLS AND TOOL CARE

For low-maintenance gardening, power tools, such as edgers, string trimmers and rotary tillers, can make quick work of your gardening chores. In fact, there are power tools now available for almost every task for the garden. You need only to determine which chores should be done manually and which by power tools. It's largely a matter of personal preference.

Power trimmers are essential if you have a hedge of 50 ft. or more. They are fast and efficient, saving a great deal of the time otherwise spent trimming with hand shears. Even if you have mowing strips, lawns look much neater if a little extra time is spent trimming and and a power edger makes this a snap. They come in gas or electric models and have blades that are short and cut vertically. String trimmers are another type of trimming tool ideal for touching up around trees and around the base of structures.

Your lawn mower is the most important piece of equipment for the lawn and it should be properly maintained. Be sure motor oil remains at the correct level and all fittings and gaskets are kept tight to prevent oil or gas from spilling onto the lawn. Keep your mower in a dry place. Drain the fuel tank for winter storage and in the spring, change the oil, clean the spark plug and refill the gas tank.

Blowers are one of the handiest of tools. These useful machines can greatly reduce time in raking leaves and saving back muscles. Leaves must be dry; otherwise, the standard garden rake will be necessary.

INDEX

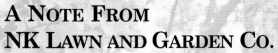

A Note From
NK Lawn and Garden Co.

For more than 100 years, since its founding in Minneapolis, Minnesota, NK Lawn and Garden has provided gardeners with the finest quality seed and other garden products.

We doubt that our leaders, Jesse E. Northrup and Preston King, would recognize their seed company today, but gardeners everywhere in the U.S. still rely on NK Lawn and Garden's knowledge and experience at planting time.

We are pleased to be able to share this practical experience with you through this ongoing series of easy-to-use gardening books.

Here you'll find hundreds of years of gardening experience distilled into easy-to-understand text and step-by-step pictures. Every popular gardening subject is included.

As you use the information in these books, we hope you'll also try our lawn and garden products. They're available at your local garden retailer.

There's nothing more satisfying than a successful, beautiful garden. There's something special about the color of blooming flowers and the flavor of home-grown garden vegetables.

We understand how special you feel about growing things—and NK Lawn and Garden feels the same way, too. After all, we've been a friend to gardeners everywhere since 1884.